GRADUATION

by Lyman Coleman

Six Sessions for Ending a Group

Serendipity House / P.O. Box 1012 / Littleton, CO 80160 / 1-800-525-9563

©1995 Serendipity House. All rights reserved.

95 96 97 98 99 /CH/ 6 5 4 3 2 1

OVERVIEW OF THIS COURSE

Session 1 / Countdown 6: SHARING OUR STORY (First Base)

Relive some of the beautiful memories of the PAST and dream a little about the FUTURE. Commit to the countdown agenda—to "birth" new groups at the close of this course.

Session 2 / Countdown 5: AFFIRMING OUR GIFTS (Second Base)

Take an inventory of your spiritual gifts and share what you discover about your qualifications for "birthing" a new group. You need a group leader, a co-leader and a host to "birth" a new group. Where do you fit in?

Session 3 / Countdown 4: SHARING OUR CONCERNS (Third Base)

Take the Needs Assessment Survey of your church and community. What does this tell you about your present small group program? What needs should you target for new groups? Who would you nominate to lead these new groups?

Session 4 / Countdown 3: DEALING WITH OUR FEARS (Home Plate)
How are you feeling about giving up the safety of your own group? Deal with your mixed emotions? Let's face it. Giving "birth" to anything is never easy. Jot down a prospect list for your new group.

Session 5 / Countdown 2: GOING-AWAY PARTY

Relax and have fun predicting some crazy things your group members might do. Then, dream a little about breaking out of the walls of your church to reach out to hurting people as you plan to give "birth" to new groups.

Session 6 / Countdown 1: COMMISSIONING

Do it any way you want, but here are two or three options for saying "good-bye" and commissioning your group to the new thing God is calling you to do. Here's to the dream.

1

To Dream the Impossible Dream . . .

GATHERING / 15 Minutes / All Together

Leader: Remember your purpose—to help your group celebrate your life together and get ready to give birth to new groups. This session has three parts: (1) Gathering/15 Minutes, (2) Bible study/30 Minutes, and (3) Countdown/45 minutes. The ice-breaker is designed to reminisce. Stop after 15 minutes and move on.

Looking Back. If you were to make a scrapbook of your life together as a group, what snapshots would you want to include in the scrapbook?

1. How did your group get started?

2. Where was the first meeting? What was it like?

3. What were you expecting when you joined the group?

4. When did you really "become" a group—where you could trust one another with your problems?

5. As you look back, would you say that you achieved your purpose?

BIBLE STUDY / 30 Minutes / Groups of 4

Leader: Pause at this point and remind the group of the purpose of this course—to help celebrate the past and to release the group to the new thing that God is calling you to do—individually or as a group.

Introduction. There are two goals in this course: (1) to celebrate what God has done in your group during your life together, and (2) to dream about the possibility of giving "birth" to a whole new series of groups for your church and community.

The Bible study time in each session is designed to help you accomplish these two goals. The Bible studies are all taken from the book of Acts—the experiences of the early church. The discussion will be guided by a questionnaire with multiple-choice options and there are no right or wrong answers, so you do not need to worry about being correct.

If you have more than 7 people in your group, we recommend that you divide into groups of 4 for the Bible study time, so that everyone can participate and you can finish the Bible study in 30 minutes. Then, regather the entire group for the last part of the session—the Countdown time. To prepare for the Countdown time, we have inserted a special box in the Countdown to help you evaluate your church and to dream about the kind of church you want to be.

Now, to get ready for the Bible study, move into groups of 4 and ask one person in each foursome to be the leader. Then, read the Scripture aloud and start with question #1 in the questionnaire.

Jesus Taken Up Into Heaven — Acts 1:1–1, NIV

1 *In my former book, Theophilus, I wrote about all that Jesus began to do and to teach ²until the day he was taken up to heaven, after giving instructions through the Holy Spirit to the apostles he had chosen. ³After his suffering, he showed himself to these men and gave many convincing proofs that he was alive. He appeared to them over a period of forty days and spoke about the kingdom of God. ⁴On one occasion, while he was eating with them, he gave them this command: "Do not leave Jerusalem, but wait for the gift my Father promised, which you have heard me speak about. ⁵For John baptized with water, but in a few days you will be baptized with the Holy Spirit.*

⁶So when they met together, they asked him, "Lord, are you at this time going to restore the kingdom to Israel?"

⁷He said to them: "It is not for you to know the times or dates the Father has set by his own authority. ⁸But you will receive power when the Holy Spirit comes on you; and you will be my witnesses in Jerusalem, and in all Judea and Samaria, and to the ends of the earth."

⁹After he said this, he was taken up before their very eyes, and a cloud hid him from their sight.

¹⁰They were looking intently up into the sky as he was going, when suddenly two men dressed in white stood beside them. ¹¹"Men of Galilee," they said, "why do you stand here looking into the sky? This same Jesus, who has been taken from you into heaven, will come back in the same way you have seen him go into heaven."

1. How do you think the followers felt when Jesus told them that he had to leave them?
a. terrified
b. excited about the new thing
c. totally confused
d. angry

2. How much of a chance would you have given the followers of Jesus at this point in going out to change the world?
a. a big chance
b. some chance
c. a little chance
d. no chance at all

3. Why do you think Jesus asked this small group to stay in Jerusalem and wait for something?
a. They couldn't make it alone.
b. to deal with their pain together
c. to help each other understand what was going on
d. to develop a strategy for spreading the message

4. What do you think the disciples did during the 10 days when they returned to the Upper Room and waited on the Holy Spirit to come?
a. unpacked their crazy, mixed-up feelings
b. told stories about the "good ol' days"
c. cried a lot about losing Jesus
d. tried to figure out what Jesus was talking about
e. experienced Christian community for the first time—as the "walking wounded ... becoming the wounded healer" (Henri Nouwen)

5. As you face the prospect of saying good-bye as a small group and moving on to the new thing God has for you, how are you feeling?
a. grief and loss
b. mixed feelings
c. anticipation for the next step in my journey
d. Hey, wait a minute, I didn't know this is what this course is all about!

6. What is the thing you are going to miss most about this group?
a. the fun
b. caring for one another
c. the Bible study
d. the times in prayer
e. getting to know people whom I will cherish for the rest of my life

7. As you start on this six-week count-down to end your group and dream about "birthing" new groups, how are you feeling right now?
a. anxious
b. confused
c. upset
d. goosebumps
e. sad
f. excited

8. How would you like to end this group in these six sessions?
a. with a big party
b. please, no tears
c. Let's remember the good times we had.
d. Let's think of it as "giving birth to new groups, not saying good-bye."

COUNTDOWN / 45 Minutes / All Together

Leader: Remind the group of the two-fold purpose of this course. In the Countdown at the close of each session, the purpose is to plan for the future—to "give birth" to new groups in your church. Regather all groups for this Countdown.

Introduction. Dream a little. What would your church be like if everyone belonged to a caring group like the one you have been in? What would it take to make this dream come true?

In the next six sessions, you will have a chance to ask these questions and dream a dream for your church. The Countdown in this session has three steps.

Step 1: Two Questions. Here are two questions for you to ask about your church and a diagram to help you answer each question.

QUESTION #1: What kind of a church are you right now? Answer this question by picking one of the four windows that best identifies your church.

Quadrant I:	Quadrant II:
SEEKER-DRIVEN CHURCH	**ASSIMILATION (PARA) CHURCH**
Targeted to reach ... • Unchurched people with no Christian commitment	Targeted to reach ... • Unchurched people who have made a Christian commitment, but don't go to church
Small Groups that appeal to ... • Felt needs • Low-level commitment • Seeker Bible study	Small Groups that appeal to ... • Spiritual growth need • Short-term commitment • Two levels of Bible study: light and heavy
This kind of church will attract secular people in search of God, but you have to meet them at the "door" as they are.	This kind of church will attract Christians who are looking for a church home where they can feel comfortable.
Quadrant III:	**Quadrant IV:**
SEEKER-FRIENDLY CHURCH	**TRADITIONAL CHURCH**
Targeted to reach ... • Churched people who grew up in the church, but have left a personal faith in Christ	Targeted to reach ... • Churched and committed Christians
Small groups that appeal to ... • Babyboomer/babybuster need • Short-term commitment • Two levels of Bible study/light and heavy	Small groups that appeal to ... • Discipleship needs • Long-term commitment • Deep Bible study
This kind of church is for church prodigals who are on their way back to God and are returning to the church for support ... and to revisit their past.	This kind of church must look at its overall purpose and mission statement if it wants to grow.

Observation: You may feel your church is a combination of one or more of these quadrants. Every church has got to minister to all four quadrants or you will miss out on some of the people who are in your church—which brings us to the second question.

QUESTION #2: Once you have identified the type of church you are, take a look at your small group program and pinpoint the people in your church who are presently in small groups. Then, answer this question,

> *"If we are going to reach out to people for new groups, who do we need to target in a new series of small groups?"*

Finish this sentence:

> *"Most of the people who are in small groups in our church are in the _____ % of our church."*

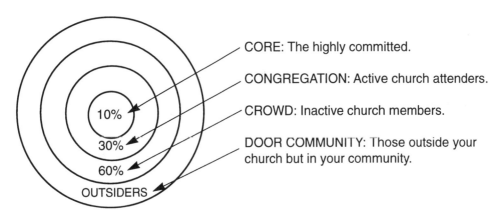

CORE: The highly committed.

CONGREGATION: Active church attenders.

CROWD: Inactive church members.

DOOR COMMUNITY: Those outside your church but in your community.

Step 2: Dream a Little. If you are a church that must focus on all four quadrants of people (Question #1), and if you want small groups for all of the levels of commitment (Question #2), what would you like your church to work on? Go around and let everyone finish the two sentences below and explain:

> *"I would like our church to be a place where ...*

> *"I would like for our church to start some small groups for people who are ...*

Step 3: My Wish. If fear, time, money or ability were removed from the equation, what would be your biggest "wish" for your church? Finish the sentence:

> *"I wish our church could ...*

Now turn these wishes into prayers to close the meeting.

2

And He Gave Some to Be ...

GATHERING / 15 Minutes / All Together

Leader: The purpose of this session is to uncover your spiritual gifts and discover where they could be put to use on a leadership team to give birth to a new small group. Start off with the spiritual gifts inventory below. Then, wait until the Countdown at the end of the session to share what you discovered about yourself in this test.

DISCOVERING YOUR SPIRITUAL GIFTS

Here is a simple test to help you identify some of your spiritual gifts. This exercise has been taken from the book *Discovering Your Spiritual Gifts*, Don Fortune © 1987 (Chosen Books/Revell, Used by permission). This test focuses on seven ministry gifts that are mentioned in Romans 12:6–8. For each question, choose the response that best describes you. You will "score" your answers at your next meeting.

1. Would you consider it more loving and caring to:
   P ❑ help a person change for the better (or)
   S ❑ invite a needy person into your home?

2. Are you more likely to find fulfillment in a:
   T ❑ teaching career (or)
   G ❑ business venture

3. To form an opinion about something, would you:
   P ❑ go by what you feel and believe already (or)
   T ❑ research it until you are confident enough?

4. Would you rather encourage people to:
   G ❑ give generously to a ministry (or)
   C ❑ minister directly to those who are hurting?

5. Would you rather:
   P ❑ pray for someone (or)
   G ❑ provide for him/her?

6. In giving advice, do you:
   P ❑ quote scripture as basic ideals
   for action (or)
   E ❑ give practical, motivational steps
   for action?

7. Would you rather:
   T ❑ train others to do a job (or)
   A ❑ delegate work to others?

8. Would you rather spend time:
   P ❑ in prayer (or)
   A ❑ organizing a Christian project?

9. Do you find that you:
   T ❑ enjoy intellectual pursuits (or)
   C ❑ daydream and fantasize a lot?

10. Would you rather:
    G ❑ financially assist an ongoing
    project (or)
    A ❑ organize the next project?

11. Would you rather participate in:
    P ❑ an intercessory prayer group (or)
    C ❑ a program to feed the poor?

12. Would you rather help someone in
    need by:
    S ❑ doing something for him/her (or)
    G ❑ anonymously giving money?

13. Would you prefer to:
    E ❑ do individual counseling (or)
    A ❑ manage a group project

14. Would you rather:
    S ❑ help set up for and serve a
    church dinner (or)
    T ❑ speak to the group after dinner?

15. If a room needed cleaning, would you:
    S ❑ get a broom and sweep it
    yourself (or)
    A ❑ figure out who is best suited
    for the job?

16. Do you encourage people:
    E ❑ by sharing your own experi-
    ences (or)
    G ❑ giving them practical assistance?

17. Would you rather work with:
    A ❑ a group (or)
    C ❑ one person at a time?

18. Would you rather:
    E ❑ give motivational speeches (or)
    C ❑ help with caring type ministries

19. Are you more attentive to:
    S ❑ people's practical needs (or)
    C ❑ how people feel?

20. At a meeting, do you feel it is more
    important to:
    S ❑ make sure the room is left in
    order (or)
    E ❑ spend time socializing?

21. Do you like to have:
    T ❑ a few select friends with similar
    interests (or)
    E ❑ lots of friends, the more the
    better

This inventory focuses on seven ministry gifts from the book of Romans:

_____Teacher (T)   _____Compassionate Person (C)   _____Perceiver (P)
_____Server (S)   _____Exhorter (E)   _____Administrator (A)
_____Giver (G)

Review these answers you checked. Count up the number of "T's" and put that number on the line above next to Teacher. Do the same for the other letters/gifts. When you are done, you will have a preliminary idea of what your ministry gifts may be.

Wait until the COUNTDOWN at the close of this session to share what you discovered about yourself from this spiritual gifts inventory.

BIBLE STUDY / 30 Minutes / Groups of 4

Leader: Remind the group of the purpose of the Bible study—to eval-uate your group and to dream together about the future of your church—based on a study of the early church in the Book of Acts.

Introduction. Remember, there are two goals in this course: (1) to celebrate what God has done in your group—PAST, and (2) to dream about the future of your church and giving "birth" to some more small groups.

The Bible study is about two disciples on their way to the temple to worship when they were suddenly confronted with a need. Have someone read the story out loud. Then, discuss the questionnaire.

In the Countdown at the close of this session, you will have a chance to talk about the people in your life who confront you with a need, and how you might be able to meet that need with a small group that targets the needs of people in your church and community.

Now, if there are more than 7 in your group, quickly move into groups of 4 and spend no more than 30 minutes in the Bible study. Then, regather for the Countdown.

Peter Heals the Crippled Beggar — Acts 3:1–10, NIV

3One day Peter and John were going up to the temple at the time of prayer—at three in the afternoon. ²Now a man crippled from birth was being carried to the temple gate called Beautiful, where he was put every day to beg from those going into the temple courts. ³When he saw Peter and John about to enter, he asked them for money. ⁴Peter looked straight at him, as did John. Then Peter said, "Look at us!" ⁵So the man gave them his attention, expecting to get some-thing from them.

⁶Then Peter said, "Silver or gold I do not have, but what I have I give you. In the name of Jesus Christ of Nazareth, walk." ⁷Taking him by the right hand, he helped him up, and instantly the man's feet and ankles became strong. ⁸He jumped to his feet and began to walk. Then he went with them into the temple courts, walking and jumping, and praising God. ⁹When all the people saw him walking and praising God, ¹⁰they recognized him as the same man who used to sit begging at the temple gate called Beautiful, and they were filled with wonder and amazement at what had happened to him.

1. Why do you think the crippled man was carried to the temple gate?
   a. It was the best place to beg.
   b. Religious people give more.
   c. He wanted to be with his buddies.
   d. He wanted to be healed.

2. Why didn't Peter and John give him a little money?
   a. They didn't have any to give.
   b. They didn't believe in giving money.
   c. They knew that the crippled man didn't need money.
   d. They wanted to help the man get to the place where he didn't need money.

3. When do you think the crippled beggar started to turn around?
   a. when he came to the temple
   b. when someone stopped to help
   c. when he heard the words of Peter
   d. when he started to get up and walk

4. As you look at your own gifts, what do you do best in helping crippled people?
   a. giving money
   b. sharing your own struggles
   c. praying with the hurting person
   d. challenging/encouraging
   e. just being present

5. If you could start a small group for the hurting people in your circle of friends, who would you like to invite?
   a. some neighbors
   b. people at the office
   c. people who struggle with one of the issues I struggle with
   d. new Christians
   e. those who are going through something that I have gone through

6. What is keeping you from starting this group?
   a. fear
   b. I don't know enough.
   c. I don't know how to invite people.
   d. I don't know what to use.
   e. I don't have someone to help me.

COUNTDOWN / 45 Minutes / All Together

Leader: This countdown is designed to help you to identify future leaders in your group for giving birth to new groups. Follow the instructions carefully.

Explain the four players of a leadership team, on page 13, who are needed to give birth to a group. They need to have this information in order to understand Step 2.

At the close of this session, assign the NEEDS ASSESSMENT SURVEY in the center section of this book for HOMEWORK.

Introduction. Before you can give birth to a small group, you have to get pregnant with the dream. In the first part of this session, you took a test to uncover your spiritual gifts. Now, we want to see what your spiritual gifts may be telling you about your role in a leadership team for giving birth to a small group.

First, review on page 13 the players who are needed on a leadership team to launch a small group: (1) Host/Hostess; (2) Co-Leader/Apprentice; (3) Group Leader; and (4) Supervisor.

Then, ask one person at a time to go through this two-step procedure for placement on a leadership team for birthing a small group in your church.

Step 1: How I See Myself. Ask this person to share what they discovered about themselves in the "Spiritual Gifts" inventory at the beginning of this session.

Step 2: How Others See You. Then, ask the others in the group to add their own observations by finishing this sentence:

> *"In the time that we have been together as a group, I have observed you as strong in _____ and I believe that you would make a good _____ in giving birth to a small group."*

When you have finished with the first person, go around again on the next person, etc. until you have gone through everyone in your group. USE THIS OPPORTUNITY TO AFFIRM THE GREAT STRENGTHS YOU SEE IN EACH OTHER ... AND HOW THESE STRENGTHS COULD BE PUT TO USE FOR THE KINGDOM.

NOTE: In the center section of this book, you will find a lengthy NEEDS ASSESSMENT SURVEY. For homework, we would like you to complete this survey before the next session. Follow the instructions on the first page, and be sure to jot down in the margin any potential leaders who you would like to nominate for leading one of these groups.

SEVEN IRREDUCIBLE MINIMUMS FOR GROUP LEADERS*

1. Every group leader must attend a 6-hour (or 6-session) training event before launching a group.

2. Every group leader must have a co-leader (or apprentice) before launching a group.

3. Every group meeting must have the three components of the three-legged stool: (a) group building, (b) Bible study, and (c) mission (the empty chair).

4. Every group leader must attend ongoing training at least once a month.

5. Every group leader is committed to the mission of giving "birth" to a new group at least once a year.

6. Every group will meet at least twice a month.

7. Every group will use curricula or materials that have been approved by the leadership team or by the pastor in charge of the group.

*Greg Bourgond, College Avenue Baptist Church, San Diego

LEADERSHIP TEAM—FOR GIVING BIRTH TO A SMALL GROUP

LEADERSHIP TEAM RESPONSIBILITIES: To give birth to a small group, three people are needed to serve on a leadership team.

HOST/HOSTESS: Strong in the gift of hospitality, and a genius at organizational details.
- committed to the seven irreducible minimums on page 12
- arrange for refreshments to be served <u>before</u> the meeting starts
- find a comfortable home or meeting place for the meeting—including rooms where the large group can sub-divide into groups of 4 for the Bible study time
- have name tags available for everyone when a visitor comes
- make sure everything is conducive for sharing—TV off, temperature comfortable, arrangements for children, etc.

CO-LEADER: An apprentice in training to become a future group leader—strong in all of the gifts of leadership.
- committed to the seven irreducible minimums on page 12
- quick to observe and solve communication problems that the leader does not see
- when the group gets over eight, able to take half of the group to another room and lead the Bible study portion of the meeting
- take charge of the group when the leader is absent
- keep the emphasis on the "empty chair"—to pray every week for new people to join the group

GROUP LEADER: Strong in leadership skills. A visionary, with a passion to reach out and multiply the church through "cell" groups.
- committed to the seven irreducible minimums on page 12
- tough and tender—tough on keeping the agenda/tender when someone needs to "unload" and share
- diligent on reporting to the supervisor or pastor in charge on the progress of the group (by phone, fax or breakfast meeting)
- the quarterback of the leadership team, calling the plays, handing off the ball, moving the ball downfield, getting over the goal line

SUPERVISOR: Strong in management skills, administration and encouragement.
- committed to the seven irreducible minimums on page 12
- strategist for multiplying groups
- tough and tender—knowing when to ask a group to graduate, but sensitive to a group that needs to stay together a little longer
- willing to meet with the group leaders at least once a month for encouragement, on-going training and support

3

Lift Up Your Eyes and Look on the Fields ...

GATHERING / 15-30 Minutes / All Together

Leader: If the group members completed the Needs Assessment Survey as homework, then you can ask them to share their results for the Gathering time. If they did NOT complete the Needs Assessment Survey, you will have to use the Gathering time for this Survey and give the group a few more minutes to complete it.

NEEDS ASSESSMENT SURVEY. In the center section of this booklet, you will find a survey for assessing the needs of your church and community. Follow these three steps if you have not completed this survey before the meeting.

Step 1: Rapid Reading of the Questionnaire. Have someone read the instructions on the first page and explain the Example shown.

Step 2: Call Out A Number. Turn to page C-4 and ask someone to read out loud the first Need (Attitude Adjustment) under the category of MEN. Then, ask everyone in your group to call out a number from 1 to 10—1 being NO NEED, 10 being GREAT NEED—for a small group in your church to address this need. (Remember, you are answering for your community and those on the fringe of your church as well as for those who attend your church.)

Step 3: Possible Leader. If the name of someone in your church immediately comes to mind as a potential leader of this group because of their "life experience," jot down their name as someone you would nominate as a potential leader.

For instance, on the issue of "Miscarriage," you might jot down Tom and Mary's names because they have gone through a miscarriage and would be qualified to lead this group.

Do not take more than 15 minutes on this survey right now. The important thing is to start thinking about needs in your church and community that might be addressed with a small group. More will be said about this in the COUNTDOWN at the close of this session.

BIBLE STUDY / 15-30 Minutes / Groups of 4
Leader: Remember the two goals of this course: (1) to wrap up your group and (2) to strategize a way to birth new groups or ministries in your church. If you had to do the Needs Assessment Survey at the beginning of the session, you need to cut back on the time for Bible study.

Introduction. In the last session, you affirmed each other's spiritual gifts, and suggested the roles you would recommend for one another in a leadership team for giving birth to a new small group. In this session, we want you to take this further and consider some of the special needs in your church and how these needs could be targeted with a small group.

The Bible study is about the early church and how they cared for one another. In the first-century church (and in many countries today) the primary need was food, and the early church reached out with food. Today, the needs of our society are so many that the church is called upon to be the church for all kinds of needs.

Quickly move into groups of 4 if there are more than 7 in your group. Then, have someone in each group read aloud the Scripture and start in on the questionnaire. Be sure to save the last 45 minutes in this session for the COUNTDOWN when all of the groups get back together for the next step in the COUNTDOWN.

The Believers Share Their Possessions — Acts 4:32–37, NIV

[32]All the believers were one in heart and mind. No one claimed that any of his possessions was his own, but they shared everything they had. [33]With great power the apostles continued to testify to the resurrection of the Lord Jesus, and much grace was upon them all. [34]There were no needy persons among them. For from time to time those who owned lands or houses sold them, brought the money from the sales [35]and put it at the apostles' feet, and it was distributed to anyone as he had need.

[36]Joseph, a Levite from Cyprus, whom the apostles called Barnabas (which means Son of Encouragement), [37]sold a field he owned and brought the money and put it at the apostles' feet.

1. Why do you think the early church did such a good job of looking after each other?
   a. They lived close together where they knew each other's needs.
   b. They were more committed to looking after each other.
   c. They had the Old Testament model where the poor were cared for.
   d. They didn't have government welfare programs, so they had to look after each other.
   e. They had small "house churches" where needs could be shared.

2. Can you say about your church (and the people in your parish), "There are no needy persons among them ..."?
   a. Well, we do have a food bank.
   b. We leave welfare to the government.
   c. We have formed a committee to look into this.
   d. No, we have failed.

3. Where do the people outside of your church go when they have a need (spiritual, physical, relational, etc.)?
   a. a professional—depending on need
   b. government agencies
   c. next door neighbors
   d. no one until it is too late
   e. I don't know because I don't have any unchurched friends.

4. Where does most of the caregiving take place in your church?
   a. the Sunday morning services
   b. through our deacons/shepherds
   c. our small groups
   d. no place

5. From the Needs Assessment Questionnaire that you took on your church (and community), what did you find out?
   a. We don't have a lot of needs in our church that we are not addressing.
   b. We really don't know what the needs are in our church.
   c. We are doing a good job at looking after the spiritual needs of our people, but not doing a lot about other needs.
   d. We have specialists who take care of immediate needs (and crisis situations), but 90% of our people do not fit into those categories and "fall through the cracks."

6. If you had to go to someone in your church with the everyday needs in your life (physical, spiritual, relational, etc.) where would you go?
   a. to my pastor/assistant pastor
   b. to my small group
   c. to one or two friends
   d. no one

 COUNTDOWN / 45 Minutes / All Together

Leader: Hopefully, you have had some experience in marketing—selling widgets from door to door, over the phone or by mail. Your experience will come in handy in explaining the concept of targeting the felt needs of people with new small groups.

Introduction. In Session 1, you started out by looking at the four quadrants and thinking about how to minister to people in all four quadrants of your church:

• A SEEKER-DRIVEN CHURCH—for unchurched/non-Christian people in your parish, but not on the roles of any church.

continued on page 17 ⟶

NEEDS ASSESSMENT SURVEY

This survey identifies 60 needs where a small group might be helpful. In the grid on the next page, these needs are divided into 10 categories. And in each category, there are six levels of need.

This survey is designed as a diagnostic instrument to help your church evaluate your small group system to see if you are reaching out to people with these specific felt needs. Some of the needs are common to all of the people in a community. Some are more specific to a particular level of commitment to Christ and the church. But all of these needs are potential entry-points for people to join a small group.

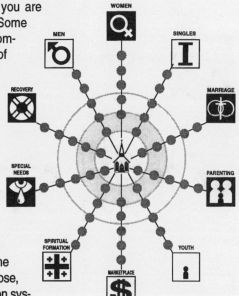

If you are taking this survey by yourself, follow these three steps: (1) read the title, subtitle and description of this need; (2) circle a number between 1 and 10—1 being NO NEED, 10 being GREAT NEED—to offer a small group to reach out to people in your church and community with this need; and (3) jot down the name of a person you think could lead this group because of their own life experience (after training, of course).

If you are taking this survey as a group, follow the instructions on page 14 in your course book. At the close, examine the subway map and small group transportation system for providing these groups as entry-points into your church.

FOR EXAMPLE:

GRIEF AND LOSS: "Getting Through the Night"
"Since he died, I've felt like half of me died, too. Why did he die and leave me so alone? I keep waking up in the night, thinking he's there. How long will this agony go on?"

1 2 3 4 5 6 ⑦ 8 9 10   *Frank Ott*
No Need   Great Need   Nomination

	Men	Women	Singles	Marriage
Trying Times	ATTITUDE ADJUSTMENT Down But Not Out	TRANSITIONS Coping With Change	LOVE AND LONELINESS Solitaire on a Saturday Night	MISCAR-RIAGE Why Our Child?
Chronic Frustration	MEN AT WORK Performance Anxiety	CINDERELLA SYNDROME When Life Is Not a Ball	PRESSURES Keeping It Together When It's Falling Apart	BALANCING ACT Winning at Work Without Losing at Home
Critical Issues	FOR MEN ONLY Issues Men Face	FOR WOMEN ONLY Issues Women Face	SEXUALITY How Do I Handle My Hormones?	DECISION-MAKING The Art of Compromise
Healthy Relationships	ACCOUNT-ABILITY Beyond Football and the Weather	ASSERTIVE-NESS Holding Your Own	DATING DILEMMA In Search of My Better Half	HONEY, I'M HOME From the Kiss at the Door to the Clothes on the Floor
Personal Growth	MASCULINITY Will the Real Jesus Please Stand Up?	REAL BEAUTY Living in a World of Glitz	CHOICES Issues Singles Face	SPIRITUALLY SINGLE Solo on Sunday
Spiritual Concepts	DISCIPLE-SHIP Being a Man After God's Own Heart	A WOMAN OF EXCELLENCE Being a Godly Woman	THE SINGLE JESUS Becoming a Whole in One	INTIMACY The Gift of Sex

Parenting	Youth	Market-place	Spiritual Formation	Special Needs	Recovery
PARENTS IN PAIN Parents of Prodigals	STRESS Surviving Day to Day	BORED AND BURNED OUT Assessing Your Career	PAIN AND SUFFERING Where Is God When It Hurts?	EMPTY NESTERS What Do We Do Now?	GRIEF AND LOSS Getting Through the Night
PARENTING A STRONG-WILLED CHILD Train Up a Child	HASSLES Getting Along With My Parents	STRESSED OUT Living in the Fast Lane	GIFTS AND CALLING What Is the Will of God for My Life?	FINANCIAL STRESS Making Ends Meet	HEALTHY HABITS Shaping Up
CHALLENGING ISSUES FOR PARENTS Special Kids With Special Needs	HOT ISSUES I've Got to Talk to Somebody	EMPLOYMENT Over-, Under- and Un-	FOR PRODIGALS ONLY Potholes on the Road Home	LIVING WITH PAIN Coping With Life's Hurts	DIVORCE RECOVERY Picking Up the Pieces
PARENTING Not Just a Stroll in the Park	BELONGING Finding Friends and Fitting In	RELATIONSHIPS AT WORK How's Your Serve?	WHOL-I-NESS With Myself, Others and God	CAREGIVERS Lifting Others Up Without Getting Down	COMING HOME Making Peace With Your Past
PARENTING ADOLESCENTS Hair, Hormones and Hassles	UP CLOSE Discovering My Real Identity	ENTREPRENEURS Going Out on a Limb	MATURING IN CHRIST Called to Discipleship	GROWING OLDER Time to Celebrate Life	ABUSE Moving Past the Pain
FAMILY TIME Making Meaningful Memories	CONFIRMATION What Do I Believe?	BUSINESS ETHICS A Christian in a Down and Dirty World	SPIRITUAL BASICS Becoming a Christian	SELF-ESTEEM Made in the Image of God	12 STEPS The Road to Recovery

MEN

ATTITUDE ADJUSTMENT: "Down But Not Out"
"Pressure is closing in on me. Too many demands. Not enough time. Money. My job. My kids. My marriage. Things are out of control and getting worse. I can't take this rat race anymore."

1 2 3 4 5 6 7 8 9 10
No Need   Great Need   Nomination

MEN AT WORK: "Performance Anxiety"
"I constantly feel like my job is on the line. I'm always afraid I'm not measuring up. Even when I'm home I worry about work."

1 2 3 4 5 6 7 8 9 10
No Need   Great Need   Nomination

FOR MEN ONLY: "Issues Men Face"
"There are some things I need to talk about, although it won't be easy. I'm sure other guys fight the same battles. We just don't tell each other. I think I'm ready to talk."

1 2 3 4 5 6 7 8 9 10
No Need   Great Need   Nomination

ACCOUNTABILITY: "Beyond Football and the Weather"
"It's about time men got together and got real. I know what's right and what I need to do. I don't need advice, but I do need a group of guys to listen, keep what I say to themselves, and hold me accountable."

1 2 3 4 5 6 7 8 9 10
No Need   Great Need   Nomination

MASCULINITY: "Will the Real Jesus Please Stand Up?"
"I get mixed messages about what a man should be—somewhere between macho and milquetoast. I know Jesus is God, but is he also someone I can look to as the ultimate man? If so, what was he like and how can I be like him?"

1 2 3 4 5 6 7 8 9 10
No Need   Great Need   Nomination

DISCIPLESHIP: "Being a Man After God's Own Heart"
"Could anyone tell me what it means to be a man of God? I'm tired of pious, sweet-Jesus talk and Sunday Christians. If I'm going to go for Christianity, I'm going all the way."

1 2 3 4 5 6 7 8 9 10
No Need   Great Need   Nomination

WOMEN

TRANSITIONS: "Coping With Change"
"My head is swimming. Last year we moved. I just went back to work. My youngest child is about to start school. Can somebody throw me a life jacket to survive all the up and down emotions that go along with change?!"

1   2   3   4   5   6   7   8   9   10   _____
No Need   Great Need   Nomination

CINDERELLA SYNDROME: "When Life Is Not a Ball"
"I never thought my life would be like this. I've had so many disappointments and unfulfilled expectations. I try so hard, but things just don't go the way I've hoped. What am I doing wrong?"

1   2   3   4   5   6   7   8   9   10   _____
No Need   Great Need   Nomination

FOR WOMEN ONLY: "Issues Women Face"
"I wish I could talk to other women about some things I can't escape. Like questions and feelings about career vs. family. About roles at home and church. And issues that require trust to even bring up."

1   2   3   4   5   6   7   8   9   10   _____
No Need   Great Need   Nomination

ASSERTIVENESS: "Holding Your Own"
"I feel like I'm always giving and always giving in. I want to be a giving person, but I have needs too. How and when do I speak up for myself?"

1   2   3   4   5   6   7   8   9   10   _____
No Need   Great Need   Nomination

REAL BEAUTY: "Living in a World of Glitz"
"I'm in a constant battle! I never feel like my hair, my shape or my clothes are quite right. Deep down I know I don't need to measure up to the glamorous stereotype, but where can I find a role model for real beauty?"

1   2   3   4   5   6   7   8   9   10   _____
No Need   Great Need   Nomination

A WOMAN OF EXCELLENCE: "Being a Godly Woman"
"What does God want me to be like? How can I apply what the Bible says about women to real life today?"

1   2   3   4   5   6   7   8   9   10   _____
No Need   Great Need   Nomination

SINGLES

LOVE AND LONELINESS: "Solitaire on a Saturday Night"
"I often go for days without a hug or meaningful conversation. Sometimes singleness is like being a social leper. How can I deal with my 'disease'?"

1 2 3 4 5 6 7 8 9 10   _____
No Need   Great Need   Nomination

PRESSURES: "Keeping It Together When It's Falling Apart"
"Panic attack ... Dirty laundry. Leaking plumbing. Broken car. Checkbook a disaster. Health problems. I'm a capable person, but how can I survive on my own?!"

1 2 3 4 5 6 7 8 9 10   _____
No Need   Great Need   Nomination

SEXUALITY: "How Do I Handle My Hormones?"
"The whole world tells me to do it. God gave me these desires. What does he expect me to do with them?! Is there anyone out there who struggles with the stuff I struggle with?"

1 2 3 4 5 6 7 8 9 10   _____
No Need   Great Need   Nomination

DATING DILEMMA: "In Search of My Better Half"
"The singles bar is a drag ... but the church scene isn't much better. I'm about ready to give up on a real relationship and forget the whole dating game."

1 2 3 4 5 6 7 8 9 10   _____
No Need   Great Need   Nomination

CHOICES: "Issues Singles Face"
"What kind of friends do I look for? How do I keep from being burned again? Should I live in community or live alone? Should I quit my job and do something exciting like go back to school or volunteer for a year overseas? What does God want me to do?"

1 2 3 4 5 6 7 8 9 10   _____
No Need   Great Need   Nomination

THE SINGLE JESUS: "Becoming a Whole in One"
"Jesus was single. Is it possible God wants me to remain single for life? How can he call singleness a 'gift'? Couldn't I serve him better with a partner? How can I be 'whole' for him now as a single?"

1 2 3 4 5 6 7 8 9 10   _____
No Need   Great Need   Nomination

MARRIAGE

MISCARRIAGE: "Why Our Child?"
"It tears me up to walk past the baby's room. Now I wish we hadn't gotten so excited and made so many plans. Why did this happen to us?! Our marriage didn't need any more stress. I'm dying inside, and I've got to talk to someone who has gone through this."

1 2 3 4 5 6 7 8 9 10 _____
No Need   Great Need   Nomination

BALANCING ACT: "Winning at Work Without Losing at Home"
"We both have so many demands for our time and energy. How can we give our best to our work without it coming at the expense of our family? I don't want to lose what we're supposed to be working for!"

1 2 3 4 5 6 7 8 9 10 _____
No Need   Great Need   Nomination

DECISION-MAKING: "The Art of Compromise"
"Why do we see things so differently?! Whether it's how to spend an evening or how to spend our income tax refund—we have a different point of view. How can we make decisions that pull us together instead of apart?"

1 2 3 4 5 6 7 8 9 10 _____
No Need   Great Need   Nomination

HONEY, I'M HOME: "From the Kiss at the Door to the Clothes on the Floor"
"We don't have a bad relationship, but why isn't marriage more fun? I want to be my spouse's best friend—as well as lover. How can I do a better job of living with the one I married?"

1 2 3 4 5 6 7 8 9 10 _____
No Need   Great Need   Nomination

SPIRITUALLY SINGLE: "Solo on Sundays"
"Since we've been married, my husband won't come to church with me. I want our children to grow up with Christian teaching, but he doesn't back me up. I love my husband and I love God. How can I please them both, and trust God to work in my husband's heart?"

1 2 3 4 5 6 7 8 9 10 _____
No Need   Great Need   Nomination

INTIMACY: "The Gift of Sex"
"The world exalts sex as the ultimate high. But we both have different needs. We'd like more romance and sizzle in our love life. How does God want us to enjoy this gift?"

1 2 3 4 5 6 7 8 9 10 _____
No Need   Great Need   Nomination

PARENTING

PARENTS IN PAIN: "Parents of Prodigals"
"Where did we go wrong? I never dreamed our son would make the choices he has. Didn't our values sink in at all? And how do we relate to him now? What should or shouldn't we say to him?"

1   2   3   4   5   6   7   8   9   10   _____
No Need   Great Need   Nomination

PARENTING A STRONG-WILLED CHILD: "Train Up a Child"
"My daughter always wants to paint outside the lines. She is really a good kid, and I love her a lot, but I don't know what to do. How do you raise a child who was born with a strong will?"

1   2   3   4   5   6   7   8   9   10   _____
No Need   Great Need   Nomination

CHALLENGING ISSUES FOR PARENTS: "Special Kids With Special Needs"
"God gave me a very special child. Now, God needs to give me the wisdom I need to raise this child. I feel somewhat alone and nobody understands."

1   2   3   4   5   6   7   8   9   10   _____
No Need   Great Need   Nomination

PARENTING: "Not Just a Stroll in the Park"
"I got into parenting before I was ready. Dr. Spock makes it sound so easy. My mother just laughs. My grandmother says everything will be OK. But I'm trying to raise my kids without a map. Please help."

1   2   3   4   5   6   7   8   9   10   _____
No Need   Great Need   Nomination

PARENTING ADOLESCENTS: "Hair, Hormones and Hassles"
"My teenager is about to drive me crazy. The music. Posters. Clothes. It's outrageous! We can't even talk about it without shouting. How can we make it through adolescence?!"

1   2   3   4   5   6   7   8   9   10   _____
No Need   Great Need   Nomination

FAMILY TIME: "Making Meaningful Memories"
"We want to live like a _real_ Christian family. Will our kids remember their childhood in a way that feels good to them and honors God?"

1   2   3   4   5   6   7   8   9   10   _____
No Need   Great Need   Nomination

C8

201

SUPPORT COURSES

SERENDIPITY EXPR...

20 courses/7 to 13 weeks
WHERE YOU HURT AND STRUGGLE

These "personal need" courses are designed for non-threatening mutual help groups with life-experience leaders. Each session has two tracks: TRACK 1—for beginner groups with easy-sharing question-naires, and TRACK 2—with deeper Bible study. A leader TRAINING MANUAL is available.

DESIGNED FOR:
- **On-going groups**
- **Retreats**
- **Special needs groups**
- **Elective Sunday school classes**

MARRIAGE ENRICHMENT COURSES
- Engaged: Are You Fit to be Tied?
- Infertility: Coping With the Pain of Childlessness
- Newly Married: How to Have a Great First Year

RECOVERY COURSES
- Addictive Lifestyles: Breaking Free
- Co-Dependency: Breaking Free From Entangled Relationships
- 12-Steps: The Path to Wholeness

PARENTING COURSES
- Blended Families: Yours, Mine, Ours
- Parenting Adolescents: Easing the Way to Adulthood
- Parents of Pre-Schoolers: From Car Seats to Kindergarten
- Learning Disabilities: Parenting the Misunderstood
- Single Parents: Flying Solo

SPECIAL NEEDS COURSES
- Compassion Fatigue: Worn Out From Caring
- Dealing With Grief & Loss: Hope in the Midst of Pain
- Divorce Recovery: Picking Up the Pieces
- Golden Years: Riding the Crest
- Midlife: The Crisis That Brings Renewal
- Single Again: Life After Divorce
- Stress Management: Finding the Balance
- Unemployed/Unfulfilled: Down, But Not Out
- Waist Watchers: Trimming Down to Size

LEADER TRAINING
- Support and Recovery Group Training Manual

What if we don't have any of these needs in our church?

Just offer these courses and see who signs up.

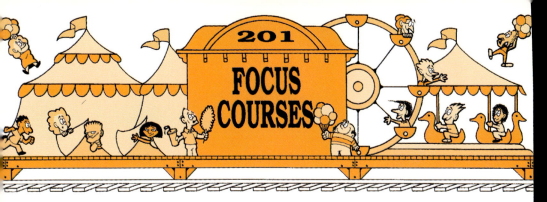

FOCUS COURSES

16 courses/7 to 13 weeks
AROUND LIFESTYLE

Pick the topic you are interested in. Reach out to others with this interest. It's called an affinity group—people with the same interest.

Each session (after the first one) has two levels or tracks: TRACK 1—for beginner groups with easy-sharing Bible questionnaires like 101 courses, and TRACK 2—with deeper Bible study. Or take both tracks and make it a 13-week course.

DESIGNED FOR:
- **Beginner Groups (track 1)**
- **On-going Groups (track 2)**
- **Sunday school classes**
- **Elective courses**
- **Retreats**

WHOL-I-NESS
Holy, Wholly, Holey, Dimensions of a Whole Person

PARENTING
Not Just a Stroll in the Park, Stages of Family Life

MAN TO MAN
Beyond Football and the Weather, Things Men Are Afraid to Talk About

SINGLES
The Secret Behind the Smile, Issues Vital to Singles

SELF-PORTRAIT
Recognizing Your Potential, Mirrors Into Knowing Yourself

STRESSED OUT
Hot, Dry and About to Crumble, Prescriptions for the Emotionally Drained

MARKETPLACE
Surviving in the Real World, Habits of a Highly Effective Christian

JESUS
Up Front and Personal, Studies on the Life of Christ

CORE VALUES
Changing From the Inside Out, Truths to Challenge Your Thinking

GIFTS & CALLING
Targeting Your Passion, Keys to a Highly Energized Life

WARFARE
Overcoming the Dragon, Studies on Spiritual Conflicts

BASICS
Confirming What I Believe, Essentials in the Christian Faith

RELATIONSHIPS
Becoming a Caring Community, Stages to Building Relationships

WOMAN TO WOMAN
Beyond the Stereotypes, Issues Women Need to Talk About

COUPLES
Making a Good Marriage Better, Skills for Effective Communications

TROUBLES
Keeping the Alligators at Bay, Strategies for Draining the Swamp

Why have 2 tracks in these courses?

So you can switch back to Beginner Bible study when new people come.

CHECK YOUR BOOK STORE OR CALL 1-800-525-9563

1 course/6 weeks
TO END A GROUP *Graciously!*

Saying "goodbye" is just as important as saying "hello," and this course is designed to help your small group feel good about ending your group meetings.

In six countdown sessions, you will reminisce over the high points in your life together and celebrate what God has done. The Bible studies are designed to discover your gifts and what God is calling you to do next.

Then, you will plan your next step in your spiritual journey and the group will support you in starting out.

Graduation completes the lifecycle of a group. As a group you will encourage each other and help one another look at the future. Your group may decide to launch a ministry or tackle a mission's project—whatever you decide, your group is there to affirm its members.

DESIGNED FOR:

- **Ending Groups**
- **Leadership Training**
- **Planning Retreats**

You are invited
to celebrate
what God has done
in your group
and
to discover
what God wants you
to do
in the future
in starting
new groups.

To this end,
here are six
countdown
planning sessions.

But we don't want to quit!

You can always be a reunion group and celebrate 3 times a year.

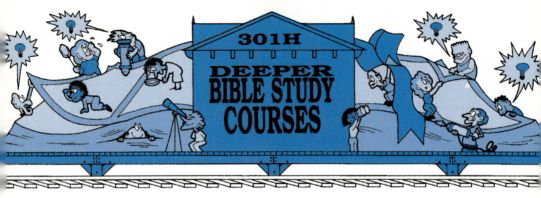

301H

DEEPER BIBLE STUDY COURSES

8 courses/1 or 2 semesters
TO COMBINE TEACHING AND GROUPS

This series is designed for churches that want to link their small groups to the teaching from the pastor, like the early church model of "temple courts ... and house to house." Each course comes with a PASTOR/TEACHER book and a STUDENT book. In the Student book, there are worksheets to complete at home and a Group Agenda for the small group meeting. Each course is designed for 1 semester, except for Corinthians and Romans which have 2 semesters.

DESIGNED FOR:
- **Church-wide groups**
- **Elective Sunday school classes**
- **Deeper Bible study groups with homework**

ONE-SEMESTER COURSES
- Ephesians (7 or 13 wks)
- Philippians (7 or 13 wks)
- James (7 or 13 wks)
- 1 John (includes 2 & 3 John, 7 or 13 wks)
- 1 Peter (1 to 10 wks)
- 1 & 2 Timothy (7 to 13 wks)

TWO-SEMESTER COURSES
- Romans (13 to 28 weeks)
- 1 Corinthians (13 to 27 weeks)

Designed for a "Two-Semester" School Year

1ST SEMESTER	
Sept. 15	Dec. 15

2ND SEMESTER	
Feb. 1	May 1

What if our pastor can't teach the passage on Sunday?

Offer the course in a Sunday school class with groups.

CHECK YOUR BOOK STORE OR CALL 1-800-525-9563

301
BIBLE STUDY COURSES

12 courses/7 to 27 weeks
TO UNDERSTAND THE BIBLE

When your group wants to go deeper in Bible study but doesn't have time for homework, this is the series for you. Each session has a built-in lap-top format with everything you need for the Bible study in a double-page layout: the TEXT of the Bible, GROUP QUESTIONS on three levels of sharing, and REFERENCE NOTES if you run across a difficult word. Beginners and Bible experts can meet on a level playing field.

DESIGNED FOR:
- On-going Groups
- Bible study groups with NO homework
- Elective courses

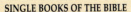

SINGLE BOOKS OF THE BIBLE
(With 2 study plans to choose from)
- 1 Corinthians (13 or 24 weeks)
- Gospel of Mark (13 or 26 weeks)
- Romans (15 or 27 weeks)
- Revelation (13 or 26 weeks)
- Miracles (13 weeks)
- Parables (13 weeks)
- Sermon on the Mount (13 weeks)
- Ministry of Jesus Christ (13 weeks)

COMBINATION BOOKS
(With 4 study plans to choose from)
- 1 Peter (8 or 10 weeks) James (8 or 12 weeks)
- 1 John (5 or 8 weeks) & Galatians (7 or 13 weeks)
- Philippians (8 or 10 weeks) & Ephesians (8 or 11 weeks)
- 1 Timothy (6 or 9 weeks), 2 Timothy (6 weeks) & Titus (4 weeks)

What is the lap-top format? Sounds like a computer!

It's everything you need for group discussion in a double-page format.

8-HOUR
or
WEEKEND
SMALL GROUP
RETREAT KIT

A Serendipity Seminar is now available for you to hold your own training day for small group leaders.

The KIT includes:
- Director's book: a 48-page, fully illustrated procedure book with minute-by-minute instructions.
- Tablet with 50 handouts for each of 4 sessions.
- Two Advertising Posters
- Ten Advertising Buttons
- Ten Solid Brass Serendipity Crosses for the commissioning service at the close.

EXTRA MATERIALS ARE AVAILABLE

IN 8 HOURS YOU WILL LEARN:
- How to start a small group
- What to do in the first few weeks
- How to get acquainted
- How to study the Bible as a group
- How to move across the disclosure scale from easy sharing to heavy sharing
- How to pray for the empty chair and reach out to new people
- How to multiply when you are ready
- How to use the Serendipity small group materials

Serendipity is the facility of making happy chance discoveries.

—Horace Walpole, 1743.

301H

DEEPER
BIBLE STUDY
COURSES

40

GRADU
CO

YOUTH

STRESS: "Surviving Day to Day"
"I have to buy my own clothes. Bum a ride. Make a C average just to stay on the team. Everybody's on my back. And my best friend didn't call tonight. Life stinks."

1 2 3 4 5 6 7 8 9 10 _____
No Need   Great Need   Nomination

HASSLES: "Getting Along With My Parents"
"In my parents' eyes, I can't do anything right. I don't look right, act right, study right, spend money right, or pick friends right. As long as I'm still at home, will I always be wrong?"

1 2 3 4 5 6 7 8 9 10 _____
No Need   Great Need   Nomination

HOT ISSUES: "I've Got to Talk to Somebody"
"My friend is pregnant. Another is talking about suicide. What do I do? School is a jungle. People get beat up. Drugs are everywhere. If my parents knew what I have to face every day, they'd freak out!"

1 2 3 4 5 6 7 8 9 10 _____
No Need   Great Need   Nomination

BELONGING: "Finding Friends and Fitting In"
"I always feel out of place. It's so hard to fit in. I don't want to come off like either a shy nerd or an obnoxious jerk. Can I be myself and still have friends?"

1 2 3 4 5 6 7 8 9 10 _____
No Need   Great Need   Nomination

UP CLOSE: "Discovering My Real Identity"
"I know I'm good at some things and not so good at others. I don't want to be weird, but I do want to be myself. What makes me unique? How can I be all that I was meant to be?"

1 2 3 4 5 6 7 8 9 10 _____
No Need   Great Need   Nomination

CONFIRMATION: "What Do I Believe?"
"It's easy to let what I hear at church go in one ear and out the other. I think it's time to know what I really believe, and really believe what I already know."

1 2 3 4 5 6 7 8 9 10 _____
No Need   Great Need   Nomination

MARKETPLACE

BORED AND BURNED OUT: "Assessing Your Career"
"My job is like a broken record. The same thing over and over again. By 10 o'clock, I'm already tired. By noon, I'm ready to go home. Is it just me ... or my work? Maybe I need an attitude adjustment."

1 2 3 4 5 6 7 8 9 10   _____
No Need   Great Need   Nomination

STRESSED OUT: "Living in the Fast Lane"
"The stress I'm under every day is incredible. Deadlines, projects, personnel—plus home and family. If I don't find a way to release some of this pressure, I'm gonna crack!"

1 2 3 4 5 6 7 8 9 10   _____
No Need   Great Need   Nomination

EMPLOYMENT: "Over-, Under- and Un-"
"For years I felt like I was in over my head. Then I didn't even have a job for awhile. And now I'm overqualified and unfulfilled! Will I ever be content?"

1 2 3 4 5 6 7 8 9 10   _____
No Need   Great Need   Nomination

RELATIONSHIPS AT WORK: "How's Your Serve?"
"I don't know which is worse—working under someone or supervising others. I've done both, and either way I've been frustrated. How can I get along better with the people I work with?"

1 2 3 4 5 6 7 8 9 10   _____
No Need   Great Need   Nomination

ENTREPRENEURS: "Going Out on a Limb"
"I was so excited to start my own business, but now I'm not so sure. Rather than working when I want to work, I'm working all the time. This is such a huge investment. I hope my dream doesn't become a nightmare!"

1 2 3 4 5 6 7 8 9 10   _____
No Need   Great Need   Nomination

BUSINESS ETHICS: "A Christian in a Down and Dirty World"
"It sounds easy on Sunday, but Monday morning the rubber hits the road. It's dog eat dog. Cut the corners. Slice the meat a little thinner and say your prayers on Sunday. Can you live like a Christian in the business world <u>and</u> try to get ahead?"

1 2 3 4 5 6 7 8 9 10   _____
No Need   Great Need   Nomination

SPIRITUAL FORMATION

PAIN AND SUFFERING: "Where Is God When It Hurts?"
"My best friend died in a car wreck. My grandfather died of cancer. My sister has MS. My little brother has learning disabilities. My parents got divorced. If God is supposed to be good and loving, how can he allow such terrible things to happen?"

1 2 3 4 5 6 7 8 9 10   _____
No Need   Great Need   Nomination

GIFTS AND CALLING: "What Is the Will of God for My Life?"
"I believe I have a gift, but I don't think God wants me to use it the way I've always wanted to. How can I be sure I'm hearing him, and how long must I wait to see what he has for me?"

1 2 3 4 5 6 7 8 9 10   _____
No Need   Great Need   Nomination

FOR PRODIGALS ONLY: "Potholes on the Road Home"
"God, I'm on my way back, but I keep hitting roadblocks. Bad habits. Temptations. I hear voices from my past reminding me of all the bad things I've done ... and telling me that I will never make it. Please be patient."

1 2 3 4 5 6 7 8 9 10   _____
No Need   Great Need   Nomination

WHOL-I-NESS: "With Myself, Others and God"
"Which areas of life do you need to work on to become a whole person: Your physical life? Vocational life? Emotional life? Relational life? Volitional life? Spiritual life? Does anyone else struggle with focusing on all these at the same time?"

1 2 3 4 5 6 7 8 9 10   _____
No Need   Great Need   Nomination

MATURING IN CHRIST: "Called to Discipleship"
"Now that I have given my life to Christ, what do I do next? I need to think through my priorities. My relationships. My goals in life. And I need a group of people to help stay the course."

1 2 3 4 5 6 7 8 9 10   _____
No Need   Great Need   Nomination

SPIRITUAL BASICS: "Becoming a Christian"
"I feel a little stupid and afraid to ask, but I didn't grow up in a church and I never really heard what it means to become a Christian. How do I get to know someone I can't see, touch or hear?"

1 2 3 4 5 6 7 8 9 10   _____
No Need   Great Need   Nomination

SPECIAL NEEDS

EMPTY NESTERS: "What Do We Do Now?"
"I guess I wasn't prepared for the kids being gone. It's like part of my identity went with them. I feel like it's half time and a whole new strategy needs to be made for the second half of life."

1 2 3 4 5 6 7 8 9 10   _____
No Need   Great Need   Nomination

FINANCIAL STRESS: "Making Ends Meet"
"I've got the mortgage. The loan to pay off. And now these credit card bills. How did I get myself into this? I could ask a relative for a loan, but I would rather die than admit I've blown it. What do I do?"

1 2 3 4 5 6 7 8 9 10   _____
No Need   Great Need   Nomination

LIVING WITH PAIN: "Coping With Life's Hurts"
"I feel like I'm dragging a ball and chain around. How can I deal each day with the pain I'm in, plus the guilt I feel for being such a burden to others?"

1 2 3 4 5 6 7 8 9 10   _____
No Need   Great Need   Nomination

CAREGIVERS: "Lifting Others Up Without Getting Down"
"I want to help any way I can, but their constant demands are so draining. How can I care for others without burning out myself?"

1 2 3 4 5 6 7 8 9 10   _____
No Need   Great Need   Nomination

GROWING OLDER: "Time to Celebrate Life"
"Others may say I'm over the hill, but I want to feel on top of the world! How can I look back with gratitude, and look ahead by passing what I've learned on to someone else?"

1 2 3 4 5 6 7 8 9 10   _____
No Need   Great Need   Nomination

SELF-ESTEEM: "Made in the Image of God"
"No matter what others do to show their love for me, I can't seem to accept it. People say that since God created me I'm special. I want to believe that, but I'm having a hard time feeling it. If I can't meet people's expectations, how can I meet God's?!"

1 2 3 4 5 6 7 8 9 10   _____
No Need   Great Need   Nomination

RECOVERY

GRIEF AND LOSS: "Getting Through the Night"
"Since he died, I've felt like half of me died, too. Why did he die and leave me so alone? I keep waking up in the night, thinking he's there. How long will this agony go on?"

1 2 3 4 5 6 7 8 9 10   _____
No Need   Great Need   Nomination

HEALTHY HABITS: "Shaping Up"
"I've tried so many diets and exercise plans. They either don't work or I don't stick with them. I hate what I see in the mirror. But what do I do? I feel like giving up."

1 2 3 4 5 6 7 8 9 10   _____
No Need   Great Need   Nomination

DIVORCE RECOVERY: "Picking Up the Pieces"
"The divorce is final, but I still feel numb. On the outside, things haven't changed that much. But on the inside, it's another matter. I feel lost. Alone with my anger. How can I ever start to heal?"

1 2 3 4 5 6 7 8 9 10   _____
No Need   Great Need   Nomination

COMING HOME: "Making Peace With Your Past"
"My parents and I have hurt each other in the past. We're losing precious time. In my heart I want to make things right—before it's too late. But I'm afraid and need some help."

1 2 3 4 5 6 7 8 9 10   _____
No Need   Great Need   Nomination

ABUSE: "Moving Past the Pain"
"The hardest thing I ever did was share my darkest secret. Now that I've dared to open up the wound, what can I do to heal the pain? I know I'm not alone, but who can help me through?"

1 2 3 4 5 6 7 8 9 10   _____
No Need   Great Need   Nomination

12 STEPS: "The Road to Recovery"
"I'm hooked, and this thing is stronger than I am. I know I need a 'Higher Power' and I know that 'Higher Power' is God. How can God help me break the stranglehold in my life?"

1 2 3 4 5 6 7 8 9 10   _____
No Need   Great Need   Nomination

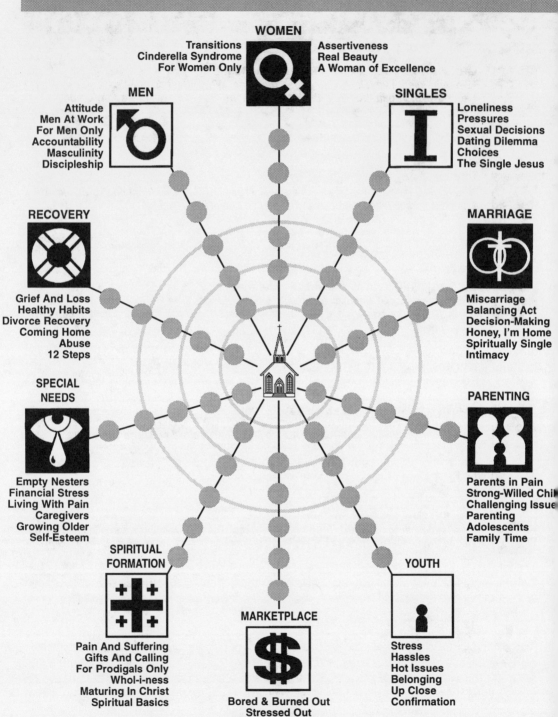

WOMEN

Transitions
Cinderella Syndrome
For Women Only

Assertiveness
Real Beauty
A Woman of Excellence

MEN

Attitude
Men At Work
For Men Only
Accountability
Masculinity
Discipleship

SINGLES

Loneliness
Pressures
Sexual Decisions
Dating Dilemma
Choices
The Single Jesus

RECOVERY

Grief And Loss
Healthy Habits
Divorce Recovery
Coming Home
Abuse
12 Steps

MARRIAGE

Miscarriage
Balancing Act
Decision-Making
Honey, I'm Home
Spiritually Single
Intimacy

SPECIAL NEEDS

Empty Nesters
Financial Stress
Living With Pain
Caregivers
Growing Older
Self-Esteem

PARENTING

Parents in Pain
Strong-Willed Chil
Challenging Issue
Parenting
Adolescents
Family Time

SPIRITUAL FORMATION

Pain And Suffering
Gifts And Calling
For Prodigals Only
Whol-i-ness
Maturing In Christ
Spiritual Basics

MARKETPLACE

Bored & Burned Out
Stressed Out
Employment
Relationships At Work
Entrepreneurs
Business Ethics

YOUTH

Stress
Hassles
Hot Issues
Belonging
Up Close
Confirmation

If you have ever ridden on a subway in a large city, you will understand the Serendipity model for small groups—bringing people from the fringe of the church to the center, and the center of the church to the fringe.

It works like a subway system with entry points and switching stations so that a person or group can travel on their "journey inward ... journey outward."

For those outside of the church and the inactive members who are on the roles of the church but never come, there are short-term, felt-need, support and recovery groups (the HEARTS on the outside of the ring).

For those who attend church, there are CIRCLE groups and DIAMOND groups. The CIRCLE groups are home groups that study the sermon from the pulpit. The DIAMOND groups start with a short-term covenant (SCROLL) that can be renewed again and again until it's time to graduate (CHALICE).

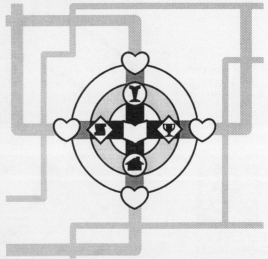

The INNER CROSS of the church (the 10% committed core and the 30% remainder of the active congregation), like a shuttle in a subway system, is designed to move people back out to the fringe to become leaders of new groups for people "at the door."

Like a good subway system, you can enter wherever you are in your spiritual journey. Those at the core can start as a Discipleship Group (BIBLE symbol); all those active in the congregation can start as a CIRCLE or DIAMOND group. Those who are inactive or "at the door," can enter through the HEART group entry-points. But wherever you start on your journey, the goal is the same—to stay on the train and move from your journey inward to your journey outward.

Periodic stations are good and necessary so that people can get off (and out) of one train and onto another, based on their need and interest.

HOW GENERAL MOTORS WOULD MARKET
DIFFERENT GROUPS FOR DIFFERENT PEOPLE

The HEARTS represent **Support** and **Recovery** Groups that target the felt needs of people on the fringe of the church or "at the door." No commitment is required to join the group. Duration is 7 to 13 weeks, after which the group can continue if they wish to make a short-term commitment to a deeper level of spiritual growth.

The INNER CROSS represents the 10% and the 30% population of the church who attend regularly and are willing to make a commitment to a group: (1) the VERTICAL BAR with the pulpit at the top and the house at the bottom represents a small group system that is based on the teaching each week from the pulpit—which is the basis for the house group study during the week; (2) the HORIZONTAL BAR represents a small group system for those who are willing to commit to be a covenant group, but do not use the teaching of the pulpit as their study material. Then, after a year or so, they can take this Graduation course to recycle into new

FOUR KINDS OF GROUPS

HEART / Support Groups • Felt needs • Short-term commitment • Seeker Bible study	**CIRCLE / Pulpit Groups** • Bible application of Sunday sermon • Cell system of multiplication
DIAMOND / Covenant Groups • Groups choose kick-off curriculum • Renew covenant if they want to continue	**BIBLE / Discipleship Groups** • Group follows some discipleship curriculum • High accountability

Serendipity House • P.O.Box 1012 • Littleton, CO 80160
1-800-525-9563

continued from page 16

- A SEEKER-FRIENDLY CHURCH—for prodigals who grew up in the church and are coming back to the church for support and help in raising their children.

- ASSIMILATION (PARA) CHURCH—for Christians who came to Christ in a para-church ministry, but have never found a church where they feel comfortable.

- TRADITIONAL CHURCH—for churched Christians who like the church the way it is, but want a small group to belong to.

Then, you were asked to evaluate the small group program in your church to see who are involved in your small groups:

- 10% CORE — highly committed
- 30% CONGREGATION — active, there every Sunday
- 60% CROWD — inactive, come on Easter and Christmas
- OUTSIDERS — untouched, broken, hurting people at the "door" of your church

In Session 2, you discovered what kind of leadership is required to launch a small group system in your church.

- HOST — with the gift of hospitality
- CO-LEADER — an apprentice in training
- GROUP LEADER — a quarterback who knows the game plan, calls the plays, hands off the ball to others and keeps the team moving the ball downfield
- SUPERVISOR—to encourage the small group leaders and keep everything on target (the seven irreducible minimums on page 12)

From the Needs Assessment Survey, you have already identified a number of areas in your church and community where a small group is needed. You may have already jotted down the name of a person who might be a leader or co-leader for this group because of their "life experience" in this area. Now, we want you to take this one step further and try to identify a leadership team for this group, consisting of: (1) group leader; (2) co-leader/apprentice; (3) host/hostess

Give each person a moment to jot down one specific group that you are willing to commit to—and who you would pick for your leadership team. Then, go around and share your dream team. Then turn these dreams into prayers.

TYPE OF GROUP _____

PURPOSE OF GROUP _____

LEADER _____

CO-LEADER OF GROUP _____

HOST FOR THIS GROUP _____

Here I Am, Lord, Send My Brother

GATHERING / 15 Minutes / All Together

Leader: Now is the time to deal with the jitters that you have when you think about giving birth to a small group. This kick-off affirmation exercise is designed to start the ball rolling.

You Remind Me Of: Ask one person in your group to sit in silence while the others AFFIRM this person by sharing one of the characteristics of Jesus that you see in this person. When you have finished with the first person, ask the next person to sit in silence while you go around on this person, etc. ... until you have gone around the entire group.

- **Jesus the Healer.** You seem to be able to touch someone's life, bind their wounds and help make them whole.

- **Jesus the Servant.** There seems to be nothing that you would not do for someone.

- **Jesus the Preacher.** You have a way of sharing your faith that is provoking, inspiring and full of hope.

- **Jesus the Administrator.** As Jesus had a plan for the disciples, you are able to organize ways of accomplishing great things for God.

- **Jesus the Leader.** Because you are a visionary, people will be willing to follow you anywhere.

- **Jesus the Miracle Worker.** You seem to defy the laws of nature in your efforts to make God's kingdom come alive.

- **Jesus the Sacrifice.** Like Jesus, you seem to be willing to sacrifice anything to glorify God.

- **Jesus the Rebel.** By doing the unexpected, you remind me of Jesus' way of revealing God in unique, surprising ways.

- **Jesus the Teacher.** You have a way of bringing the Scripture to life in a way that offers hope and truth.

- **Jesus the Critic.** You have the courage to say what needs to be said, even if it isn't always popular.

BIBLE STUDY / 30 Minutes / All Together

Leader: Keep to your focus in this course—to help the group say goodbye and plan a strategy for birthing new groups or ministries in your church. Use this Bible study as a stepping stone to the COUNT-DOWN at the end of this session.

Introduction. Do you remember the time when you graduated from elementary school ... or junior high ... or high school ... or college? You probably remember a lot of the good feelings of accomplishment. But you probably had a lot of jitters—about the future and the unknown. It is always that way in life when graduation comes around.

In three weeks (or three sessions) you will be graduating from this small group and moving on to the new thing that God is calling you to do.

In the Bible study in this session, you will meet two people. One you know well as the great apostle in the early church—the apostle Paul. The other is an unknown layperson whom God used in a mighty way.

Move into groups of four now and have someone read the Scripture out loud. Then follow the questions for your discussion. Call time after 20-30 minutes and regather for the Countdown.

Saul's Conversion — Acts 9:1–6,10–19, NIV

Meanwhile, Saul was still breathing out murderous threats against the Lord's disciples. He went to the high priest ²and asked him for letters to the synagogues in Damascus, so that if he found any there who belonged to the Way, whether men or women, he might take them as prisoners to Jerusalem. ³As he neared Damascus on his journey, suddenly a light from heaven flashed around him. ⁴He fell to the ground and heard a voice say to him, "Saul, Saul, why do you persecute me?"

⁵"Who are you, Lord?" Saul asked.

"I am Jesus, whom you are persecuting," he replied. ⁶"Now get up and go into the city, and you will be told what you must do."

¹⁰In Damascus, there was a disciple named Ananias. The Lord called to him in a vision, "Ananias!"

"Yes, Lord," he answered.

¹¹The Lord told him, "Go to the house of Judas on Straight Street and ask for a man from Tarsus named Saul, for he is praying. ¹²In a vision he has seen a man named Ananias come and place his hands on him to restore his sight."

¹³"Lord," Ananias answered, "I have heard many reports about this man and all the harm he has done to your saints in Jerusalem. ¹⁴And he has come here with authority from the chief priests to arrest all who call on your name."

¹⁵But the Lord said to Ananias, "Go! This man is my chosen instrument to carry my name before the Gentiles and their kings and before the people of Israel. ¹⁶I will show him how much he must suffer for my name."

¹⁷Then Ananias went to the house and entered it. Placing his hands on Saul, he said, "Brother Saul, the Lord—Jesus, who appeared to you on the road as you were coming here—has sent me so that you may see again and be filled with the Holy Spirit." ¹⁸Immediately, something like scales fell from Saul's eyes, and he could see again. He got up and was baptized, ¹⁹and after taking some food, he regained his strength.

1. How would you compare your conversion to the conversion of Saul (Paul)?
   a. Mine was a lot more gradual.
   b. I didn't go blind or anything like that.
   c. My experience was quite different, but just as real.
   d. I'm still trying to figure out what happened to me.
   e. I'm on my way back to God and I still have a lot of questions.

2. How do you think Ananias felt when God told him to go visit the home of Judas and lay hands on Saul?
   a. "God, you must be kidding!"
   b. thrilled at what God would do
   c. inadequate, knowing Saul was a great Bible scholar
   d. totally confused

3. Who is the Ananias in your life whom God used to introduce you to Jesus?
   a. my parent or pastor
   b. a concerned friend
   c. a number of people—over time
   d. a stranger

4. What circumstances did God use to bring you and "Ananias" together?
   a. We were friends.
   b. I was going through a crisis.
   c. This person invited me into his circle of Christian fellowship.
   d. I was a prodigal and this person still accepted me.

5. Do you think Saul could lead a small group right after he was converted?
   a. no—absolutely not
   b. well, maybe after a few weeks
   c. sure—if it was a group for seekers
   d. absolutely—but I would want a "Barnabas" as his co-leader

6. What about Ananias? Would he make a good small group leader?
   a. No—he doesn't have the leadership qualities.
   b. He would be a better co-leader.
   c. It depends upon the kind of group—he would be a lousy Bible study group leader, but a great recovery group leader.
   d. I don't know enough about Ananias.

COUNTDOWN / 45 Minutes / All Together

Leader: In this countdown, encourage everyone to fill out their prospect list, using the suggestions in the Introduction below. If group members started to think in terms of teaming up in the last session, ask the teams to meet as teams to work together on the prospect list.

Introduction. In the last session, you created a dream leadership team to give birth to a new group. Now, we want you to take this one step further and create a prospect list for possible candidates for this group. Here are people to consider:

- **A Friend:** Who is someone you would like to invite because this person is a special friend who NEEDS a group? Jot down this person's name.

- **Affinity:** Who is someone who shares a common interest, concern or hobby, such as a love for mountain climbing? This "affinity" or commonality often becomes a "bond" that would encourage this person to join your group if <u>you</u> invited them.

- **Felt Need:** Who is someone who has the same life situation or need that you have? Maybe you are both single. Or both of you have gone through a miscarriage and have a need for support on this issue.

- **Extended Family:** Who is someone with a need for a family because they live far away from their own family—and need a support system? They may not be active in church, but you would like to have them in your "extended" family.

On the lines below, jot down five or six names of people who immediately come to mind as you have read this list. Like a good Amway salesperson, call this list your PROSPECT LIST. Put this list on your refrigerator door and pray every day for these people until you have invited them into your group.

Now, share with your group what you have done. Then, commit this list to God in prayer.

MY PROSPECT LIST

_____ _____

_____ _____

_____ _____

NOTE: In the next session, you will talk about curriculum. You may want to call SERENDIPITY and ask them to send a set of their curriculum. Call 1-800-525-9563.

SESSION

5

It's Been Good

GATHERING / 15 Minutes / All Together

Leader: This is the next to the last session in the Countdown. You will be making final decisions in this session about the future, and planning the kind of celebration for your final meeting as a group. Start off with this fun exercise. (You may already have done this exercise when your group first started, but now you will know a whole lot more about one another—and should get a good laugh doing it again).

Predictions. Knowing each other as you do, try to predict the person in your group who is most likely to accomplish the following. First, read through the list of accomplishments. Then, ask everyone to call out the name of the person you feel will be most likely to do this.

Read the next item and again call out your predictions until you have gone through the list.

THE PERSON IN OUR GROUP MOST LIKELY TO:

_____ take Joe Montana's place in the Hall of Fame

_____ become a movie star like_____

_____ skateboard across the country

_____ open a charm school for Hell's Angels

_____ become a famous model for Parisian negligees

	run a dating bureau for middle-aged bachelors
_____	run a dating bureau for middle-aged bachelors
_____	rise to the top in the Mafia
_____	be the first woman to win the Indianapolis 500
_____	get busted for skinny-dipping in the public park
_____	win the lottery and retire to the South Sea Islands
_____	join the French Foreign Legion
_____	make a fortune on pay toilet rentals
_____	be the saleswoman of the year for aerobic gear
_____	write a best-selling novel based on all the dates they had
_____	set a world record for blowing bubble gum
_____	get listed in the *Guinness Book of World Records* for the messiest car

BIBLE STUDY / 30 Minutes / Groups of 4

Leader: This Bible study is going to be hard on small groups from traditional churches that like to paint "within the lines." But it is important to see the significance of this story if your small group is going to break out of the confines of your church in "birthing" new groups. Just be open.

Introduction. In the past sessions, you started to think about your "parish"—and the needs of people on the fringe and beyond the doors of your church.

You are going to meet two kinds of people in this Bible story. One came from the 10% CORE of the church. The other was on the outside—at the DOOR. Try to identify with both people, and try to apply the lesson you learn to the small group that you are planning to "birth."

Move quickly into groups of 4 and ask someone to read the Bible story out loud. Then, move into the questionnaire ... and be sure to save the last 45 minutes at the close of this session for the COUNTDOWN.

Cornelius Calls for Peter — Acts 10:1-23, NIV

10At Caesarea there was a man named Cornelius, a centurion in what was known as the Italian Regiment. *²He and all his family were devout and God-fearing; he gave generously to those in need and prayed to God regularly. ³One day at about three in the afternoon he had a vision. He distinctly saw an angel of God, who came to him and said, "Cornelius!"*

⁴Cornelius stared at him in fear. "What is it, Lord?" he asked.

The angel answered, "Your prayers and gifts to the poor have come up as a memorial offering before God. ⁵Now send men to Joppa to bring back a man named Simon who is called Peter. ⁶He is staying with Simon the tanner, whose house is by the sea."

⁷When the angel who spoke to him had gone, Cornelius called two of his servants and a devout soldier who was one of his attendants. ⁸He told them everything that had happened and sent them to Joppa.

Peter's Vision

⁹*About noon the following day as they were on their journey and approaching the city, Peter went up on the roof to pray.* ¹⁰*He became hungry and wanted something to eat, and while the meal was being prepared, he fell into a trance.* ¹¹*He saw heaven opened and something like a large sheet being let down to earth by its four corners.* ¹²*It contained all kinds of four-footed animals, as well as reptiles of the earth and birds of the air.* ¹³*Then a voice told him, "Get up, Peter. Kill and eat."*

¹⁴*"Surely not, Lord!" Peter replied. "I have never eaten anything impure or unclean."*

¹⁵*The voice spoke to him a second time, "Do not call anything impure that God has made clean."*

¹⁶*This happened three times, and immediately the sheet was taken back to heaven.*

¹⁷*While Peter was wondering about the meaning of the vision, the men sent by Cornelius found out where Simon's house was and stopped at the gate.* ¹⁸*They called out, asking if Simon who was known as Peter was staying there.*

¹⁹*While Peter was still thinking about the vision, the Spirit said to him, "Simon, three men are looking for you.* ²⁰*So get up and go downstairs. Do not hesitate to go with them, for I have sent them."*

²¹*Peter went down and said to the men, "I'm the one you're looking for. Why have you come?"*

²²*The men replied, "We have come from Cornelius the centurion. He is a righteous and God-fearing man, who is respected by all the Jewish people. A holy angel told him to have you come to his house so that he could hear what you have to say."* ²³*Then Peter invited the men into the house to be his guests.*

1. What immediately strikes you in this Bible story?
   a. the spiritual desire of the Gentile centurion
   b. the attitude of Peter toward Gentiles
   c. the eagerness of the Gentile to seek God
   d. the willingness of Peter to break the rules

2. Why do you think this story got into the Bible?
   a. Cornelius was the first Gentile to become a Christian.
   b. It was a turning point in the church.
   c. To teach us not to put limits on God.
   d. Peter had to justify what he did.

3. Who would it be harder for you to accept in your group right now?
   a. Peter—with his very religious mindset
   b. Cornelius—with his meek mindset
   c. We could accept either.

4. If the other person showed up at your group, what would you do?
   a. keep right on going as we are
   b. stop and let the person tell his story
   c. ask the person to join another group
   d. We would probably have trouble with both persons.

5. If you were going to start a group for the outsiders (like Cornelius) who do not know a whole lot about the Christian faith, what would you do differently?
a. I would change the focus/agenda.
b. I would let everyone explain their spiritual story so that we could get to know one another.
c. I would move immediately into the Bible—deep spiritual things.
d. I would let the group decide.

6. As you think about the people in your world, who are some of the people whom you have written off?
a. people with something against the church
b. very religious types
c. the "rich and famous"
d. New Age counterfeits
e. anybody who is over 30
f. those always asking for a handout
g. anybody who sleeps with his girlfriend

7. What kind of Bible study would you use if a newcomer who didn't know a lot about the Bible joined your group?
a. fill-in-the-blank Bible study with right answers to look up in the Bible
b. start off with a lecture and then let newcomers ask questions if they didn't understand the answers
c. use open-ended questions with multiple-choice options, no right or wrong answers
d. send newcomers to a catechism class where they get grounded in the Word

NOTE: All four approaches to Bible study are valid and needed, but we have discovered the open-ended/multiple-choice approach is best for beginner groups that have a variety of spiritual levels. The "no right answer" approach allows the group to share on an equal playing field.

COUNTDOWN / 45 Minutes / All Together

Leader: Take some time at the close of this session to plan a final celebration or going-away party for next week—the last session. If you plan to use the Serendipity cross in the commissioning service, call Serendipity right away for these crosses.

Introduction. Take a few minutes at the beginning of this time to let everyone report on what you are doing about your dream to "give birth" to a new group. Then, spend a little time looking over the various curriculums that you may want to use in birthing your group. The fold-out brochure in the center of this book will show you the various courses that Serendipity offers. Or you may want to use other curriculums.

If you have time, have someone explain the lifecycle of a group that is illustrated in the conveyor belt on page 27. You may also want to study the four-step process of courses on this conveyor belt. A full explanation of these courses can be found in the fold-out brochure in the center of this book.

At the close of the meeting, spend some time planning for the last session next week. You may want to change the setting and meet as a group in the church chancel or at a retreat setting—where you can commission one another.

Serendipity has a special "Jerusalem cross" that we have adopted as our cross for commissioning people. If you would like to use this cross, call our office at 1-800-525-9563.

Step 1: Reporting in. Go around and let everyone explain what you have done so far to give "birth" to your group.

Step 2: Serendipity Lifecycle and Bible Study. Study the box on the next page, especially the principles behind the approach to Bible study that we recommend in the "birthing" period of a small group.

Step 3: Planning Your Last Session. Decide what you are going to do next week—or at your last session—to celebrate and commission one another to the new thing God is calling you to do.

WHY DO WE DO BIBLE STUDY DIFFERENTLY?

Like any other relationship, getting to know one another in a small group is important, but not difficult.

In the Serendipity model for a group, we like to explain that there are four stages in the LIFECYCLE of a group: (1) Birthing stage (101) where you get to know one another, (2) Continuing stage (201) where you move on as a group, (3) Maturing stage (301) where you get into heavy-duty Bible study, and (401) Graduating stage—where you release each other to give "birth" to new groups.

BASEBALL DIAMOND / 101 COURSES

The Birthing Stage looks like a baseball diamond. The goal of the group is to get to home plate or *koinonia* (the Greek word for bonding in the New Testament).

To get to home plate, the small group needs to move around the three bases of sharing: (1) First Base—HISTORY GIVING—telling your story to one another; (2) Second Base—AFFIRMATION—learning to say "thank you for sharing" and affirming one another with appreciation, and (3) Third Base—GOAL SETTING—sharing your needs and goals, and letting your small group affirm you in your goals.

BIBLE STUDY FOR BEGINNER GROUPS / 101

In the first few weeks of a new group (when the group is just getting acquainted), the approach to Bible study needs to be very easy for newcomers who do not know a whole lot about the Bible and may feel uncomfortable in the typical "right answer" catechetical Bible study. (How would you feel if you were a newcomer in a group ... and everybody else in the group knew a lot more about the Bible than you did?)

This is the reason Serendipity offers a 101 Series of Bible study courses with ...

- OPEN-ENDED QUESTIONS—with multiple-choice options like a question-naire—and no right or wrong answers.

- TWO-PART QUESTIONNAIRE—starting with a Bible story and slowly moving across the disclosure scale into "My Story" ... with the "shirt off" question at the end.

- TIGHT AGENDA—with three parts carefully designed to start off easy in the (1) Gathering time with coffee; then, move into (2) Bible study, and close with (3) Caring time—for sharing and prayer.

- FEARLESS FOURSOME—moving into groups of 4 during the Bible study time so that everyone can participate.

- EMPTY CHAIR—bringing up an empty chair in the prayer time to remind you that your group is always open to newcomers.

TWO TRACKS TO CHOOSE FROM IN 201 BIBLE STUDY COURSES

But you ask, "What do we do when God answers our prayer and brings us a new person for our group ... and we have moved to the second stage of our lifecycle?"

The answer is in the TWO TRACKS in all of the 201 Bible study courses: (1) Track 1—simple, easy-sharing Bible study like 101 courses, and (2) Track 2—deeper Bible study for heavy-duty stuff.

So ... Motorcycle Mama shows up at your Bible study group. You have already finished your 101 get-acquainted stage and you are into heavy-duty Bible study. What are you going to do for Motorcycle Mama?

You are going to say to the group at the beginning of the night: "Tonight, we are going to use the Bible study from Track 1. It is the same topic. You spend two or three weeks in Track 1 ... and then move over to Track 2 again.

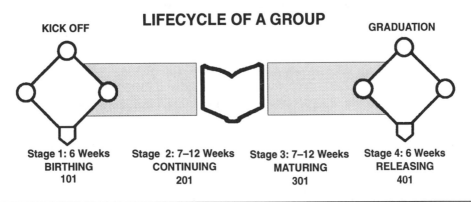

LIFECYCLE OF A GROUP

KICK OFF   GRADUATION

Stage 1: 6 Weeks	Stage 2: 7–12 Weeks	Stage 3: 7–12 Weeks	Stage 4: 6 Weeks
BIRTHING	CONTINUING	MATURING	RELEASING
101	201	301	401

DEPTH BIBLE STUDY COURSES / 301

Now your group is ready for the deepest level of Serendipity Bible study—301. We have two versions: (1) No homework, and (2) With homework—and teaching from the pulpit. You can take your pick.

But you ask again, "What do we do when Motorcycle Mama shows up at the meeting?" And the answer is in the three-part agenda that is in the Group Sharing Questions in all of these courses: (1) **To Begin**—simple, child-like questions to bring the new person up to speed; (2) **To Go Deeper**—open-ended questions where there are no right or wrong answers, and (3) **To Close**—caring questions about your life and needs for prayer.

GRADUATION / 401

This brings us to where you are at this point in your small group journey, ready to graduate and give "birth" to new groups. On the LIFECYCLE belt, this is the second baseball diamond. This is what you have been doing in the last five sessions—going around the bases a second time: (1) First Base—sharing OUR STORY as a small group; (2) Second Base—affirming one another, but in greater depth because you know each other so well; and (3) GOAL SETTING—sharing what God is asking you to do in the next stage of your journey.

Next week, you will have the final meeting of your group. The best way to describe this final meeting is to compare it to the Catholic definition of "community."

A COMMUNITY FOR LIFE

To become a member of a "community" in the Catholic tradition, you must go through a year or more as a novice. During that year, you learn what your "community" is all about. At the completion of your novitiate, you are invited to wed yourself to your community for the rest of your life. You actually put on a wedding ring to symbolize the fact that you are wedded to this community.

You may meet from time to time if your mission requires it, but this is not normal. You have given your life to this community. You do not have to meet each week to be a community. YOU ARE A COMMUNITY.

Next week (or the next session) will be the last time you will meet to celebrate what God has done. Then, you will wed yourselves to one another for the rest of your lives. You have become, in the best sense of the word, a Christian Community.

SESSION

6

Bon Voyage

GATHERING / 15 Minutes / All Together

Leader: You may have to work backwards in planning this last session. How much time will you need for the Commissioning Service at the end? Then, how much for the Bible study? Then limit the Gathering time to what you have left.

Children's Zoo. How would you describe your experience in this small group? Choose one of the animals below that best describes how your experience in this group has affected your life. Then share with the group.

WILD EAGLE: because you have helped to heal my wings, and taught me how to soar again

TOWERING GIRAFFE: because you have helped me to hold my head up and stick my neck out, and reach over the fences I have built

PLAYFUL PORPOISE: because you have helped me to find a new freedom and a whole new world to play in

COLORFUL PEACOCK: because you have told me that I am beautiful; I've started to believe it, and it's changing my life

SAFARI ELEPHANT: because I have enjoyed this new adventure, and I am not going to forget it ... or this group; I can hardly wait for the next safari

continued on next page

LOVABLE HIPPOPOTAMUS: because you have let me surface and bask in the warm sunshine of God's love

LANKY LEOPARD: because you have helped me to look very closely at myself and see some of the spots, and you have told me it's OK to be this way

DANCING BEAR: because you have taught me to dance in the midst of pain, and you have helped me to reach out and hug again

ROARING LION: because you have let me get down off my mountain, roll in the grass, and not worry about my mane

ALL-WEATHER DUCK: because you have helped me to celebrate life—even in stormy weather—and to sing in the rain

 ## BIBLE STUDY / 30 Minutes / Groups of 4
Leader: As you plan the agenda for this session, start by reserving 45 minutes for the last part—the final Countdown. This may mean cutting the Bible study short to make time for your closing experience.

Introduction. In the first session in this course, you started off with the Scripture challenge in Acts 1:8: *"... and you will be my witnesses in Jerusalem, and in all Judea and Samaria, and to the ends of the earth."*

If you compare these circles with a map of the Holy Land, you would have the same four circles of outreach that we have talked about in this course as described in Acts 1:8:

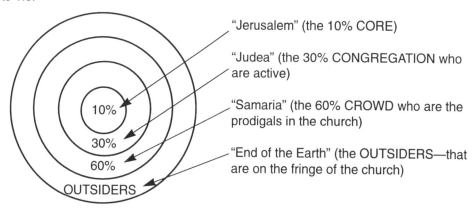

"Jerusalem" (the 10% CORE)

"Judea" (the 30% CONGREGATION who are active)

"Samaria" (the 60% CROWD who are the prodigals in the church)

"End of the Earth" (the OUTSIDERS—that are on the fringe of the church)

It is interesting that this Scripture occurs in Antioch in Syria—at the "end of the world" as far as the people at headquarters were concerned. It is also interesting that it was from this outpost—made up of new converts from the mission field on the fringe of the church—that God sent out Barnabas and Saul on the first missionary journey.

In this Bible story, use this opportunity to examine your own strategy for sending off your "Barnabas and Saul" to "birth" new groups.

Barnabas and Saul Sent Off — Acts 13:1–3, NIV

13 *In the church at Antioch there were prophets and teachers: Barnabas, Simeon called Niger, Lucius of Cyrene, Manaen (who had been brought up with Herod the tetrarch) and Saul. ²While they were worshiping the Lord and fasting, the Holy Spirit said, "Set apart for me Barnabas and Saul for the work to which I have called them." ³So after they had fasted and prayed, they placed their hands on them and sent them off.*

1. Why do you think God chose this small group in Antioch to launch the first missionary journey (instead of the church headquarters)?
   a. It was merely coincidental.
   b. They were following the leading of the Holy Spirit.
   c. They were a bunch of outcasts from the fringe of the church.
   d. They didn't know to "paint inside the lines."

2. How do you think the leadership back in Jerusalem felt when they heard what these guys were doing?
   a. thrilled
   b. embarrassed
   c. angry that they didn't follow protocol
   d. They probably didn't hear about it until later.

3. Why do you think the small group chose two people to send out instead of one?
   a. companionship
   b. They had different gifts: Paul was a hot head, Barnabas an encourager.
   c. It was coincidental.

4. As you think about sending out some members of your small group to give "birth" to new groups, what is your greatest concern for these people?
   a. keeping the faith
   b. keeping the vision
   c. keeping their personal walk with Christ
   d. keeping in touch with you for support

5. As one who is going to lead or co-lead a new group, how would you describe your emotions right now?
   a. a nervous wreck
   b. pregnant with excitement
   c. delivery room jitters
   d. Ask me next week.

6. If you could say one word of encouragement to those who are going to be new leaders, what would it be?
   a. I'll be praying for you.
   b. Call me anytime.
   c. You can do it.
   d. It's OK to fail.

COUNTDOWN / 45 Minutes / All Together

Leader: We are giving you two options for this final commissioning service (and you are free to make up a third option of your own). You may want to move to an appropriate location for this commissioning time.

Option 1: CIRCLES OF LOVE. "... So after they had fasted and prayed, they placed their hands on them and sent them off." Here are three steps to follow in practicing this Scripture commissioning experience.

- **Step 1:** Draw in your chairs real tight or sit on the floor in a circle, close together.

- **Step 2:** Ask one person to start out by finishing this sentence and explaining:

    "I feel God is calling me to ..."

- **Step 3:** When this person has finished explaining, ask this person to be commissioned by the group in one of three ways: (1) kneeling in the center of the group with the others laying their hands on this person's shoulders, (2) standing in the center of the group with the others gathering around in a football huddle, or (3) holding out his or her hands in the center of the group while the others hold on to the person's hands ... AND ONE OR TWO PEOPLE PRAY for the whole group.**

** If you are using the Serendipity cross, have one person tie this cross around their neck before the prayer.

Option 2: GIFT GIVING. This takes a little longer, but it is a beautiful, beautiful way to express your love and appreciation for one another. Follow these three steps.

- **Step 1:** Ask everyone to sit in silence and ask themselves this question, "If I could give something of myself to each person in this group ... that expresses my feelings right now for them, what would I want to give each person ... that they could keep for the rest of their lives." (This is for keeps.)

- **Step 2:** Still in silence for five to six minutes, take out your purse, or wallet ... or things in your pockets ... and try to find symbols or tokens of the real thing you would like to give this person: For instance:

    ❏ a fishing license—to remember the time we went fishing together ... or want to go in the future

    ❏ picture of my family—to remember the camping trip we took together

    ❏ a ticket stub to a concert—to remember the music that we share in Christ

    ❏ a band-aid—for the "little hurts" that come along in your work with kids

    Remember, you need ONE gift (a different gift) for each person—a token or symbol of the real gift.

- **Step 3:** Ask one person to sit in silence while the others go around and explain their gift and hand it to this person. The person who receives the gift is to say "Thanks." Nothing more.

Repeat this procedure until everyone in your group has been given their gifts. In the giving and receiving of gifts, you are able to say two things: (1) What I have appreciated most about you ... and, (2) What I want you to keep as a token of our friendship ... for the rest of your life.